Dot Marker Books for Toddlers

Easy Big Dots, best for dot markers, bright paint daubers and coloring activity for kids

Book Series: Dot Markers for Toddlers Activity Book 1

By: Marie Max House

This book

belongs to

_____

About this book:

It's designed for toddlers who are learning the coloring activity, let them do a fun dot activity, dab markers or paint. Each page comes with a scissor/paper-cutter guide line so you can take of the paper and hand it over to your toddler to enjoy and learn.

- 25 Cute Animal Illustrations
- Big Guided Dots
- Glossy Lamination Cover to protect from light spills
- Early Mental Development Activity for your toddler
- Fun, Quiet and Relaxing activity for your kid and you
- Large 8.5 x 11 inch white pages to make marker ink look bright
- Let your toddler Discover mostly cute animals, insects and few objects inside
- Perfect gift for little grandchildren or other toddlers
- Best suited for age 18months – 48months (2-4 year old)

Suggested Way to Use this Dot Marker Activity Book:
Please remember involving toddlers early on in art and craft activities enhance early brain development and boosts kids creativity. In order to use this activity book to the best we recommend using it as a **3 in 1 activity book.**

1. Let your kid do one dot page a day
2. Use safe scissors and guide your toddler by holding their hand and doing a scissor activity to cut off a page
3. Remove any sharp object like scissor and let your little one have their fun with dot markers on cute drawings
4. Store this paper, as the art created by your little one will improve with time, once you keep handing them over the same paper
5. Congratulate the little one on completing a dot activity
6. Once they have gone through the whole book, it's time to hand-over the same semi dot marker colored illustrations you stored and have them color it again.
7. You can try changing the tool they use for coloring this time, may be this time they use a thinner marker, or a crayon.

We call it the **3 in 1** learning philosophy
Scissor + Dot Marker + Coloring (SDC)

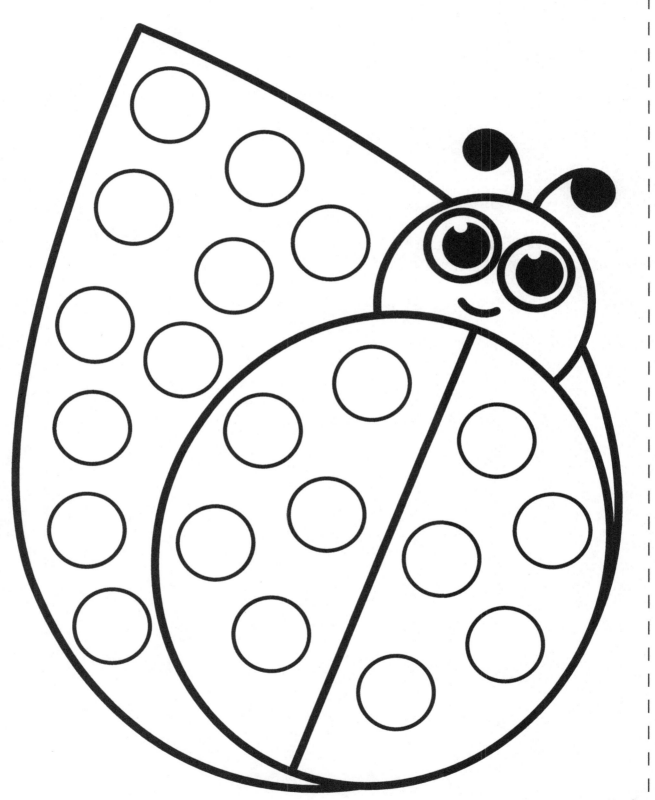

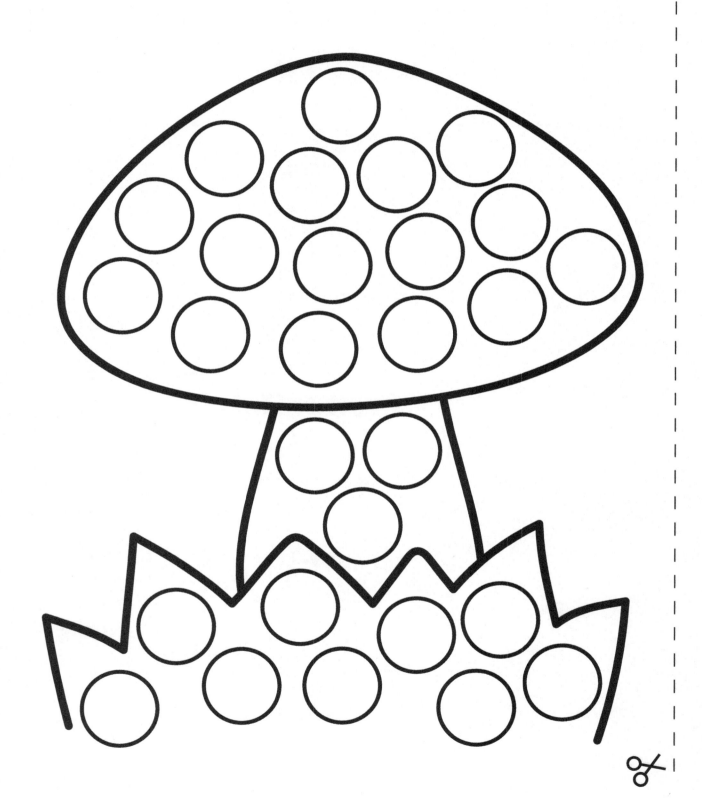

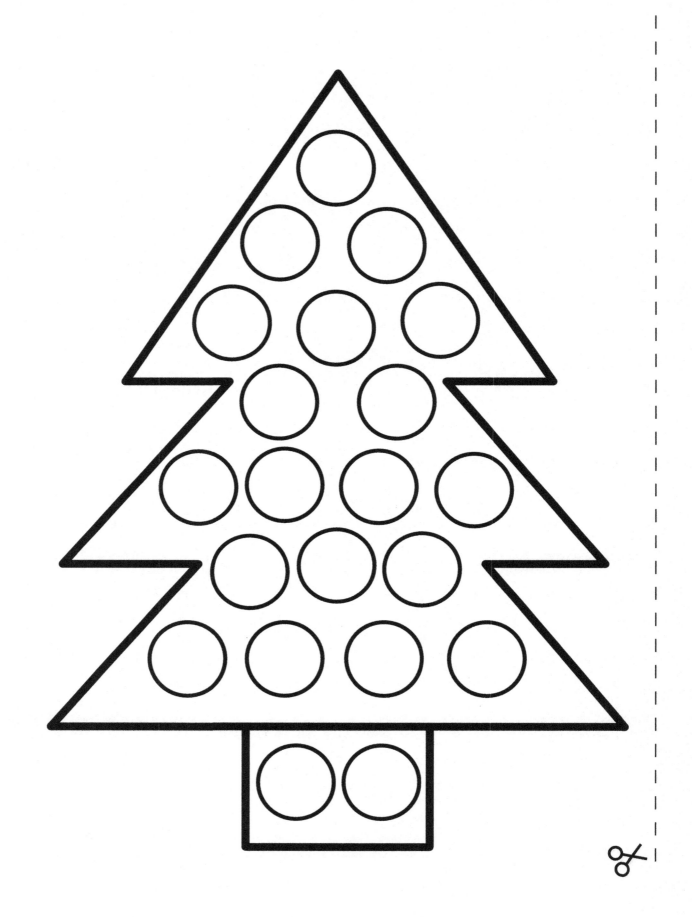

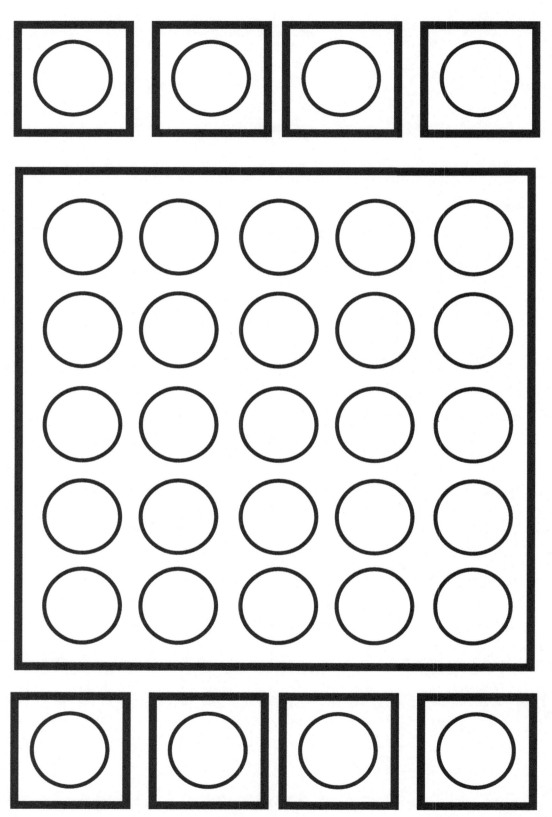

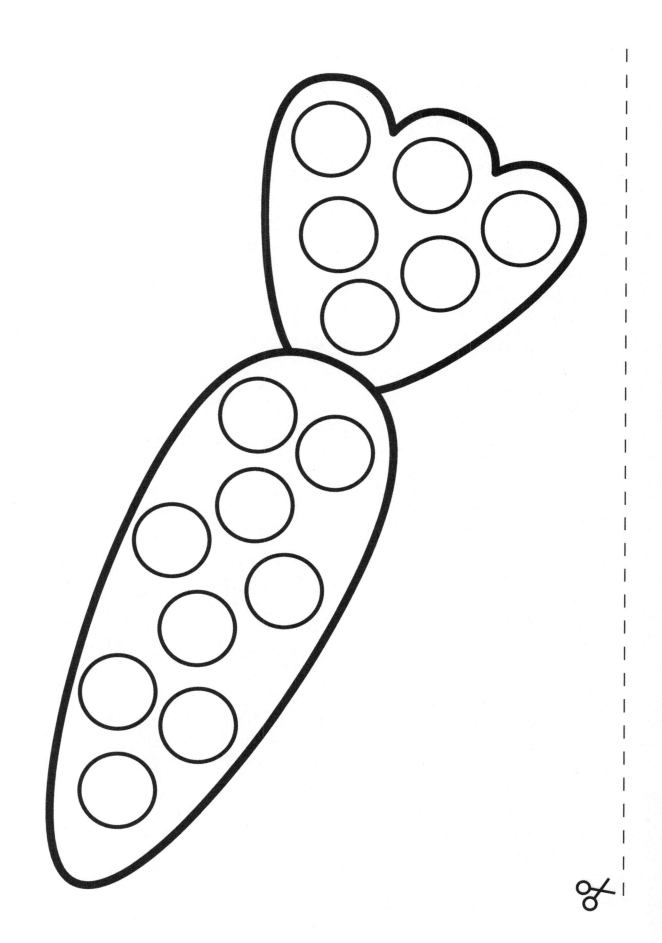

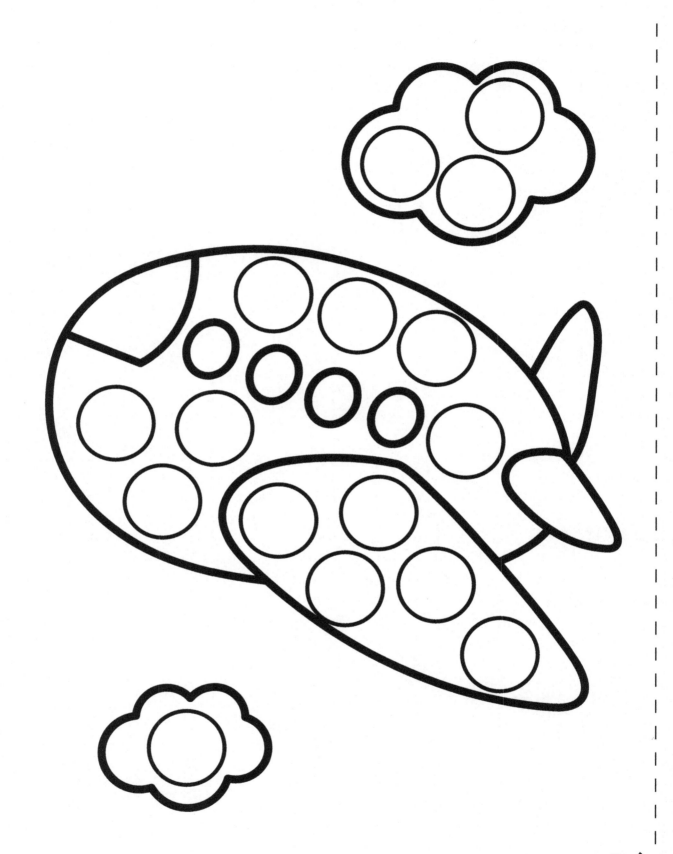

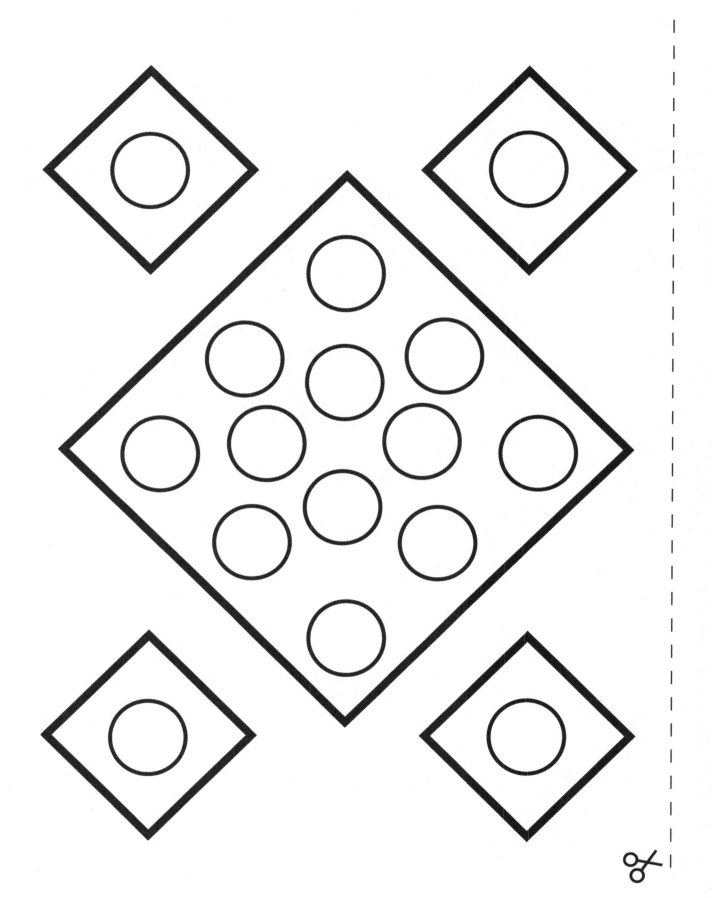

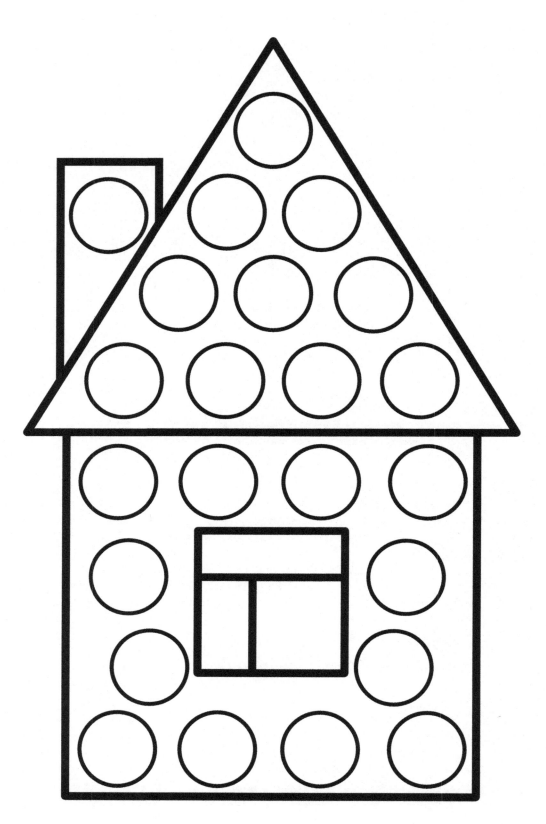

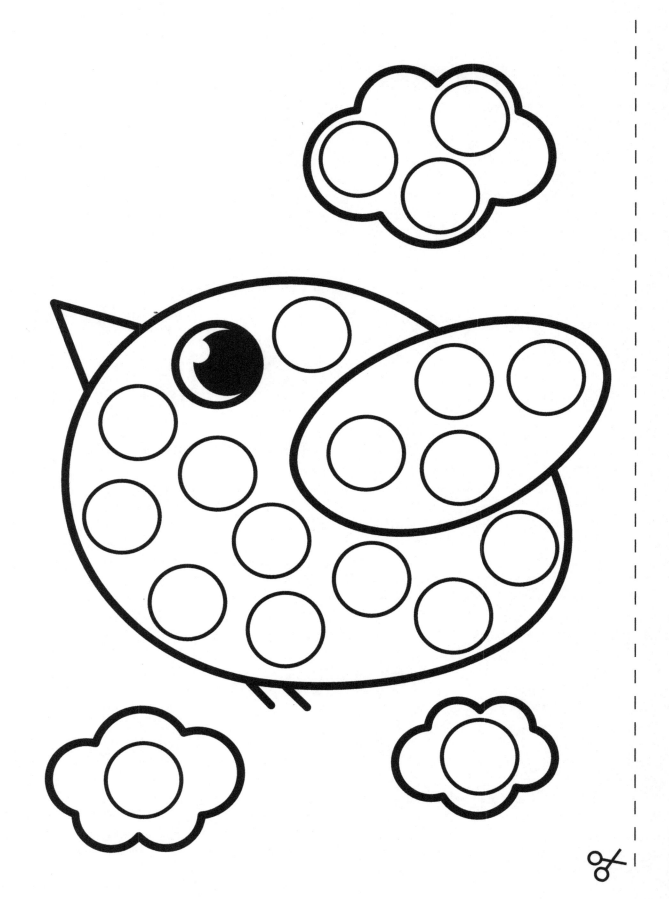

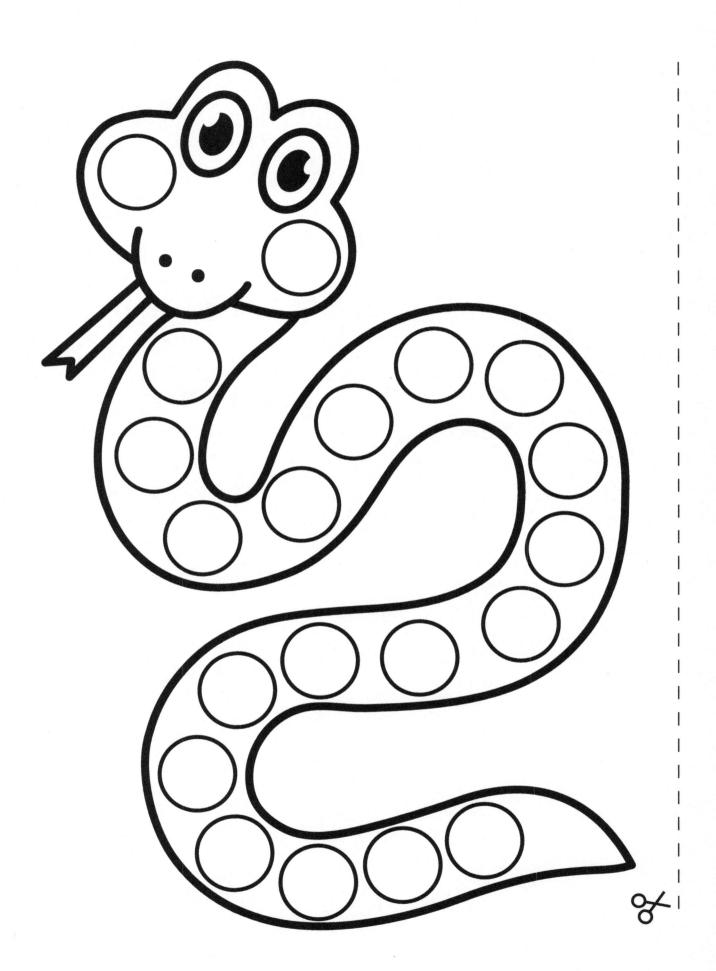

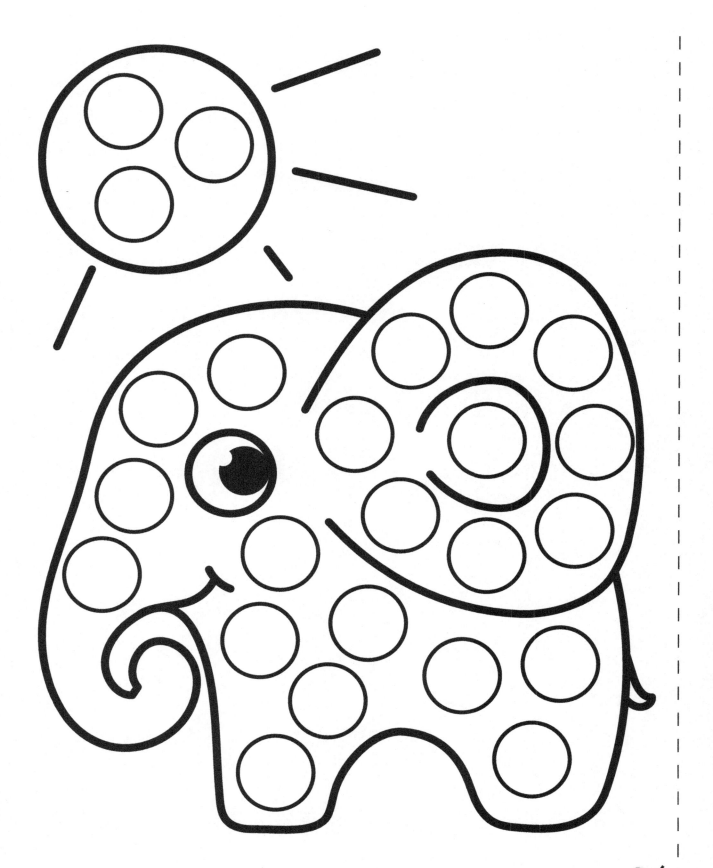

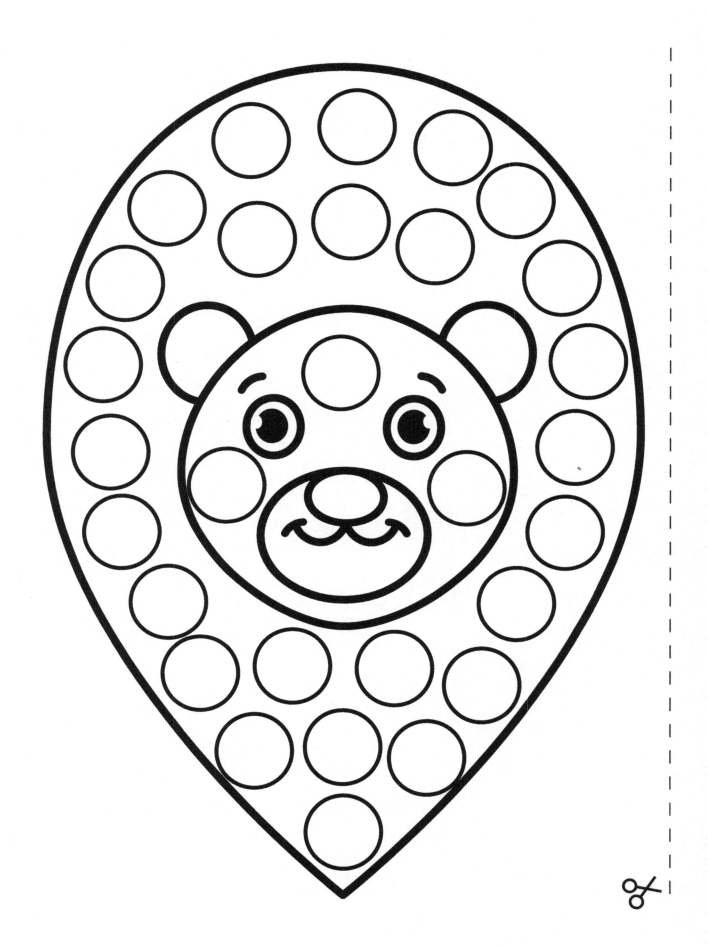

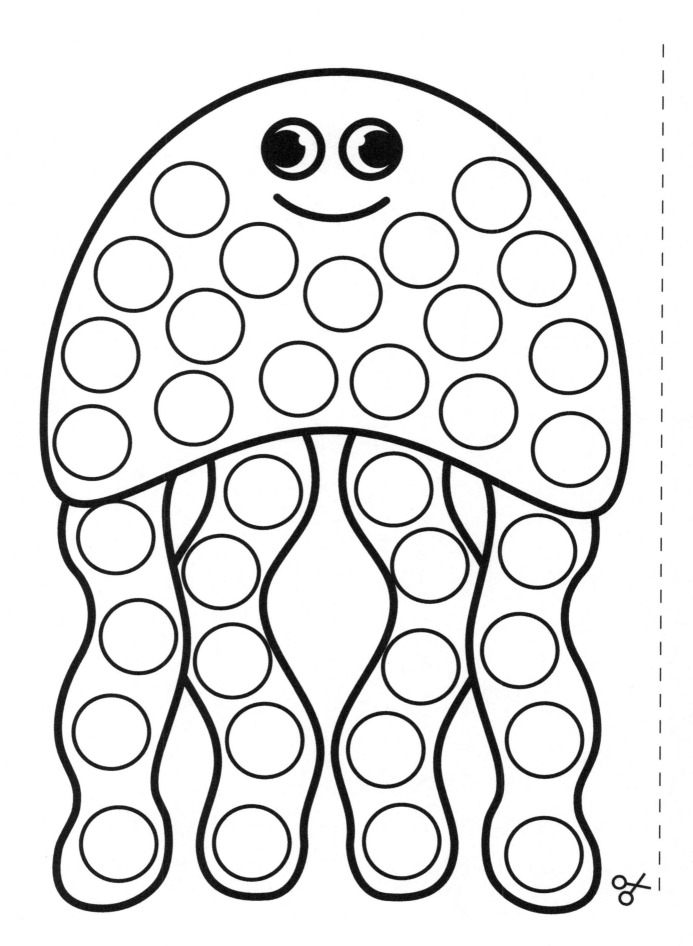

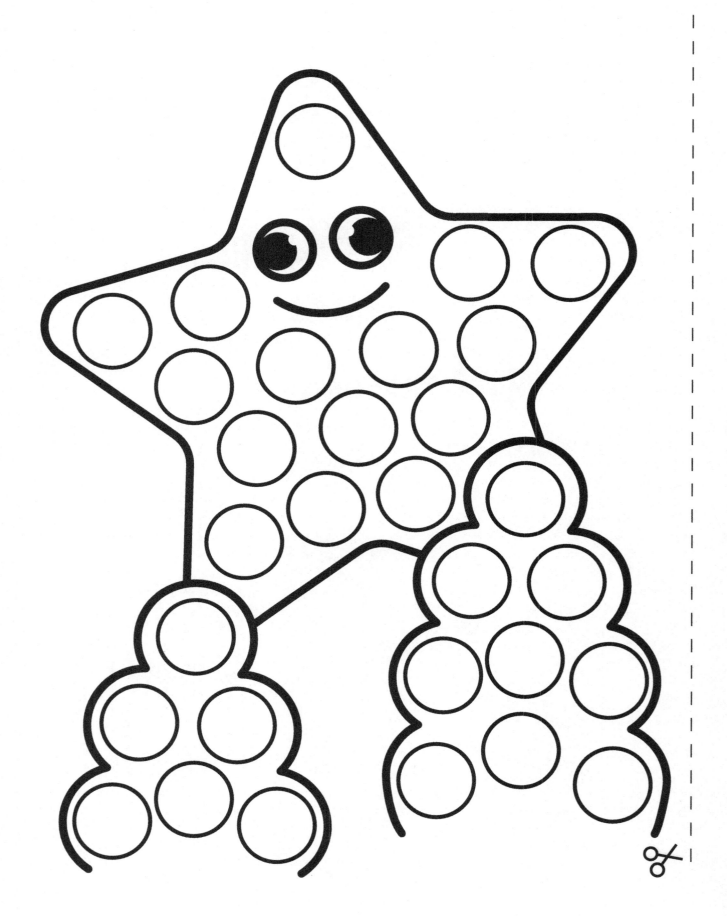

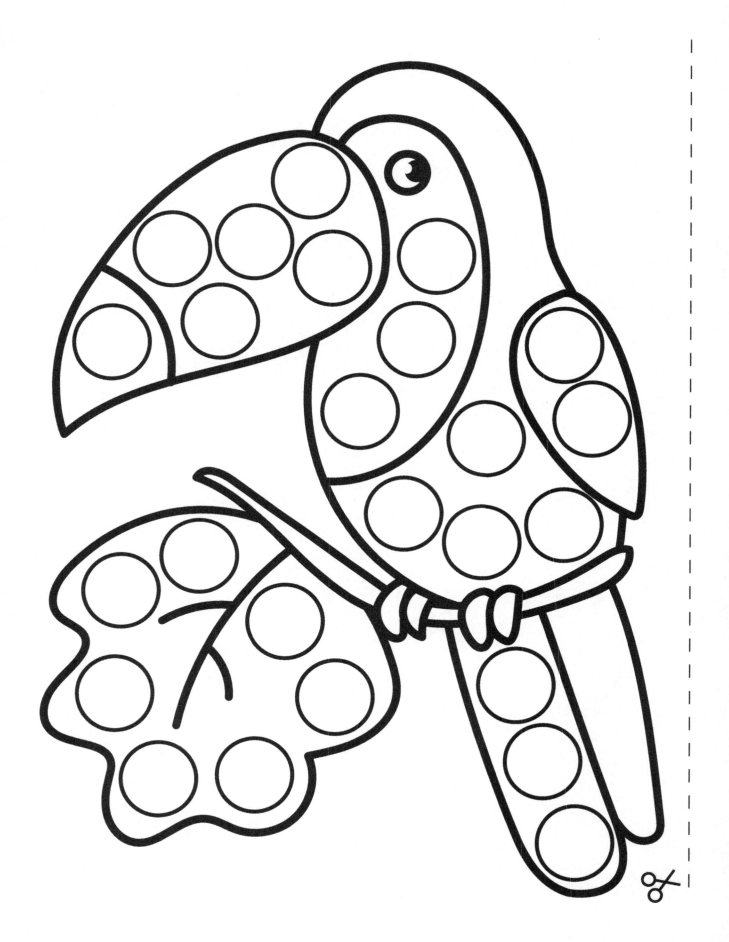

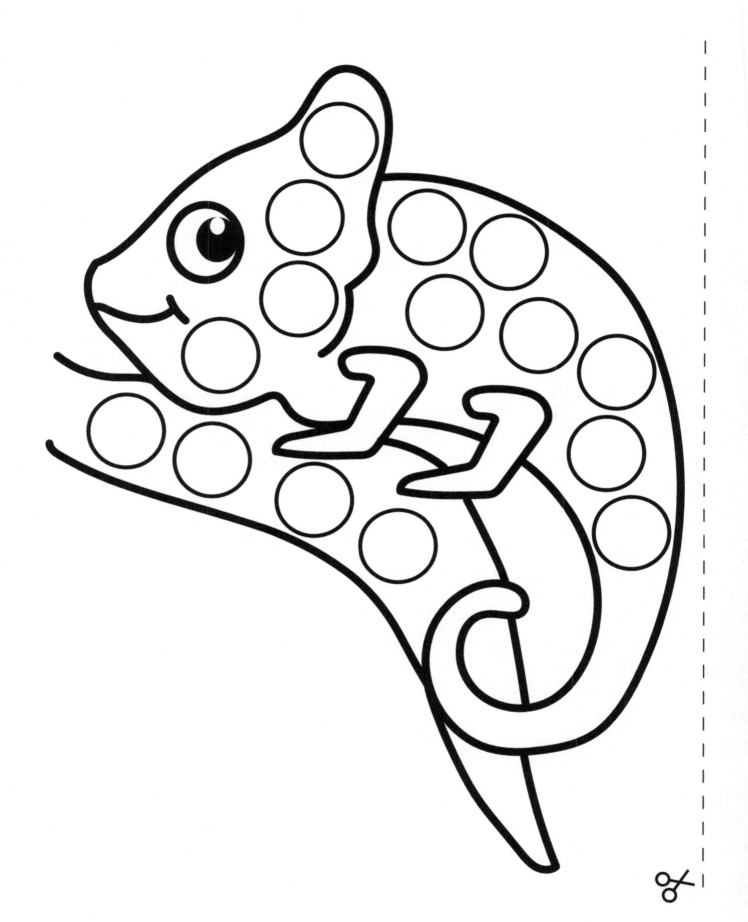

If you can still read this with this much colors, trust us, your little one has created a master piece. It's time to reward them.

We request you to please carefully cut off this page and present it to your little one. In the next edition we plan to print the certificate as the back cover so it stays robust and laminated, and ready to be framed or hanged on wall.

CONGRATULATIONS

★ **Creative Artist**

This certificate is awarded to

_____

For the completion of "Dot Marker Books For Toddlers" book 1 ,

By

Marie Max House

Made in the USA
Las Vegas, NV
07 December 2024